# Shaun White

**ABDO**
Publishing Company

by **Sarah Tieck**

Big Buddy BOOKS
Buddy Bios

 PRINTED ON RECYCLED PAPER

Coordinating Series Editor: Rochelle Baltzer
Contributing Editors: Heidi M.D. Elston, Megan M. Gunderson, BreAnn Rumsch, Marcia Zappa
Graphic Design: Maria Hosley
Cover Photograph: *Getty Images*: Kevork Djansezian.
Interior Photographs/Illustrations: *AP Photo*: Greg Baker (p. 19), Gerry Broome (p. 25), Paul Drinkwater/NBCU Photo Bank via AP Images (p. 26), Darryl Dyck/The Canadian Press (p. 29), Jae C. Hong (p. 5), Colin E. Braley (p. 7), Peter Dejong (p. 13), Jeff McIntosh, CP (p. 17), Thomas Kienzie (p. 17), Sean Kilpatrick, CP (p. 23), Ryan Pearson (p. 20), Ryan Remiorz/The Canadian Press (p. 17), Reed Saxon (p. 13), Robert Skinner, CP (p. 17); *Getty Images*: Al Bellio (p. 11), Theo Wargo/WireImage (p. 15); *Shutterstock*: Barry G. Hurt (p. 9), steba (p. 15).

### Library of Congress Cataloging-in-Publication Data

Tieck, Sarah, 1976-
 Shaun White : Olympic champion / Sarah Tieck.
   p. cm. -- (Big buddy biographies)
 ISBN 978-1-61613-979-7
 1. White, Shaun, 1986---Juvenile literature. 2. Snowboarders--United States--Biography--Juvenile literature. I. Title.
 GV857.S57T54 2011
 796.93'9092--dc22
 [B]
                          2010013424

Shaun
White

# Contents

Olympic Star . . . . . . . . . . . . . . . . . . . . . . . 4

Family Ties . . . . . . . . . . . . . . . . . . . . . . . . 6

Growing Up . . . . . . . . . . . . . . . . . . . . . . . 8

Training Wheels . . . . . . . . . . . . . . . . . . . 12

Half-Pipe Dreams . . . . . . . . . . . . . . . . . . 14

The Olympic Games . . . . . . . . . . . . . . . . 16

Big Break . . . . . . . . . . . . . . . . . . . . . . . . 18

Famous Athlete . . . . . . . . . . . . . . . . . . . 21

Victory Lap . . . . . . . . . . . . . . . . . . . . . . 22

Off the Slopes . . . . . . . . . . . . . . . . . . . . 27

Buzz . . . . . . . . . . . . . . . . . . . . . . . . . . . 28

Snapshot . . . . . . . . . . . . . . . . . . . . . . . 30

Important Words . . . . . . . . . . . . . . . . . . 31

Web Sites . . . . . . . . . . . . . . . . . . . . . . . 31

Index . . . . . . . . . . . . . . . . . . . . . . . . . . 32

# Olympic Star

Shaun is a two-time Olympic gold medalist.

Shaun White is a famous snowboarder and skateboarder. He has won **competitions** at the X Games and the Winter Olympics. Shaun is a very talented **athlete**.

Oregon

California

Nevada

PACIFIC OCEAN

Arizona

San Diego

N
W — E
S

MEXICO

# Family Ties

Shaun Roger White was born in San Diego, California, on September 3, 1986. Shaun's parents are Cathy and Roger White. Shaun's older brother is Jesse. His older sister is Kari.

Shaun's family supports his love and talent for snowboarding. They can all snowboard! His mother was the last to try it.

## Did you know...

As a baby, Shaun had heart surgery twice. And as a child, he wore leg braces at night. Even with these setbacks, Shaun showed a talent for sports at a young age.

7

# Growing Up

Shaun grew up in Southern California. His mother was a waitress. His father worked as a city employee.

The Whites enjoyed many sports and activities. They lived near the ocean. So, Shaun's parents wanted him to learn how to surf.

**Did you know...**

Shaun was named for his dad's favorite professional surfer, Shaun Tomson.

Southern California is known for its good surfing beaches.

Shaun tried surfing. But, soon he wanted to try another sport. Shaun discovered he liked skiing and was good at it.

Shaun skied very fast. When he was six, his parents got him a snowboard. They thought this would help him go slower and stay safe. But, Shaun learned quickly and snowboarded fast, too!

The Whites often traveled to the mountains to snowboard. They camped in their van to save money.

Snowboarders may go very fast.
Some do jumps and other tricks.

# Training Wheels

Growing up, Shaun also took an interest in skateboarding. When Shaun was nine, he began to work with famous skateboarder Tony Hawk! Tony said Shaun had talent.

Soon, Shaun began **competing** in both snowboarding and skateboarding. In the cold months, he practiced snowboarding. In the warm months, he practiced skateboarding.

Shaun uses similar body movements in skateboarding and snowboarding.

# Half-Pipe Dreams

Over time, Shaun became serious about snowboarding. He practiced **tricks** and jumps for several hours each day. When Shaun was 13, he became a **professional** snowboarder. He traveled to **competitions** around the world!

Shaun began attending a school in Carlsbad, California. The school allowed him to work on his own and spend more time snowboarding. He hoped to go to the Olympics someday.

Shaun learned to do snowboarding jumps and tricks in a half-pipe. This is a U-shaped area with walls made of snow.

Shaun was younger than most other professional snowboarders when he became well known.

15

# The Olympic Games

    The Olympic Games are a worldwide sports **competition**. They happen every two years. Each time, they switch between summer sports and winter sports.

    People from many countries compete to win Olympic events. First-place winners receive gold **medals**. Silver medals are given to second-place winners. And, third-place winners receive bronze medals.

Figure skating (*left*) and ski jumping (*right*) are two popular events at the Winter Olympics. Snowboarding first appeared as an Olympic event in the 1998 Olympic Games.

Swimming (*left*) takes place during the Summer Olympics. Other summer events include track and field (*right*) and gymnastics.

# Big Break

In 2006, Shaun's dream came true. He went to the Olympics in Torino, Italy! He snowboarded for Team USA. Shaun **competed** in the half-pipe event. He showed off his movements and did some **tricks**. The competition was **challenging**. But, Shaun won the gold **medal**!

Shaun was so excited to win a gold medal in Torino that he cried.

Shaun won the gold medal for vert skateboarding.

# Famous Athlete

Many people had watched Shaun win his first Olympic gold medal. This made him even more famous for his snowboarding skills.

At the same time, Shaun was building a name for himself in skateboarding. In 2007, he won his first skateboarding gold medal at the X Games. He was the first person to win titles at both the Summer and Winter X Games!

# Victory Lap

In 2010, Shaun traveled to Vancouver, British Columbia, Canada. He went to **compete** in his second Winter Olympics.

Shaun is known for doing very high jumps. He is also famous for inventing new moves.

In Vancouver, Shaun **competed** in the half-pipe event as he had in Torino. He won his second Olympic gold **medal**!

After this, Shaun was considered one of the world's best snowboarders. Many people liked his new ideas and bold moves.

Shaun is an important member of Team USA. And, his friendly personality makes him a popular athlete.

Shaun was interviewed by Jay Leno on *The Tonight Show with Jay Leno* in 2010.

Did you know...
Many snowboarders love spending time in the mountains. But, Shaun likes to be in the city.

# Off the Slopes

To keep improving his skills, Shaun spends a lot of time practicing. He works out to stay in top condition.

Shaun also attends public events and meets fans. Reporters **interview** him for magazines and television.

Shaun spends free time with his friends and family. He likes to watch television and go out to dinner.

27

# Buzz

Shaun plans to **compete** in more skateboarding events. And, he is considering competing in snowboarding at the 2014 Winter Olympics.

Fans are excited to see what's next for Shaun White! Many believe he has a bright **future**.

Shaun is known mostly for snowboarding. He wants to become more famous for skateboarding, too.

# Snapshot

★**Name**: Shaun Roger White

★**Birthday**: September 3, 1986

★**Birthplace**: San Diego, California

★**Turned professional**: 1999 (snowboarding)
2003 (skateboarding)

★**Olympic medals won**: 2 gold

# Important Words

**athlete** a person who is trained or skilled in sports.

**challenging** (CHA-luhn-jihng) testing one's strength or abilities.

**competition** (kahm-puh-TIH-shuhn) a contest between two or more persons or groups. To compete is to take part in a competition.

**future** (FYOO-chuhr) a time that has not yet occurred.

**interview** to ask someone a series of questions.

**medal** an award for success.

**professional** (pruh-FEHSH-nuhl) working for money rather than for pleasure.

**title** a first-place position in a contest.

**tricks** skillful actions.

# Web Sites

To learn more about Shaun White, visit ABDO Publishing Company online. Web sites about Shaun White are featured on our Book Links page. These links are routinely monitored and updated to provide the most current information available.

## www.abdopublishing.com

# Index

awards **4, 18, 19, 20, 21, 24, 30**

California **6, 8, 9, 14, 30**

Canada **22, 24**

education **14**

Hawk, Tony **12**

Italy **18, 19, 24**

Leno, Jay **26**

Olympic Games **4, 14, 16, 17, 18, 21, 22, 24, 28, 30**

Russia **28**

Tomson, Shaun **9**

*Tonight Show with Jay Leno, The* (television show) **26**

White, Cathy **6, 7, 8, 10, 27**

White, Jesse **6, 7, 8, 10, 27**

White, Kari **6, 7, 8, 10, 27**

White, Roger **6, 7, 8, 9, 10, 27**

X Games **4, 21**